To Chuck Wasserburg
Best Wishes

[signature]
Edinburgh May 96.

RED LETTER DAY

Books by Tom Pow

POETRY

Rough Seas (Canongate, 1987)
The Moth Trap (Canongate, 1990)
Red Letter Day (Bloodaxe Books, 1996)

ANTHOLOGY

Shouting It Out (Hodder & Stoughton, 1995)

TRAVEL

In the Palace of Serpents: An Experience of Peru
(Canongate, 1992)

Red Letter Day

TOM POW

BLOODAXE BOOKS

Copyright © Tom Pow 1996

ISBN: 1 85224 368 6

First published 1996 by
Bloodaxe Books Ltd,
P.O. Box 1SN,
Newcastle upon Tyne NE99 1SN.

Bloodaxe Books Ltd acknowledges
the financial assistance of Northern Arts.

Cover printing by J. Thomson Colour Printers Ltd, Glasgow.

Printed in Great Britain by
Cromwell Press Ltd, Broughton Gifford, Melksham, Wiltshire.

*for Julie and Cameron
and Jenny*

Acknowledgements

Acknowledgements are due to the editors of the following publications in which some of these poems first appeared: *Cencrastus, Chapman, Event* (Canada), *Lines Review, Northwords, Orte* (Switzerland), *Poetry Canada, Poetry Ireland, The Scotsman, Stand,* and *Under Cover* (Mainstream, 1993). Several poems were broadcast in *Poetry Now* on BBC Radio Four as part of Poetry Live in 1991.

'A Horse in the House' by the Peruvian poet Wáshington Delgado ('Un Caballo en Casa'), is from his book *Reunión elegida* (Selgusa Editores). The pregnancy poems in section II were written during the Gulf War.

I am grateful to the Scottish Arts Council for a Writers Bursary which enabled me to visit Alastair Reid at his home in Samaná in the Dominican Republic, and also Peru and Brazil, the settings for the poems in the first section of this book; to Greg Hollingshead and the English Department of the University of Alberta; to the Leighton Studios at the Banff Centre in Alberta; and to all who showed me friendship and hospitality while I was working on this book. I would also like to thank Dumfries and Galloway Education Authority and Dumfries Academy in particular for their support.

Contents

11   Loving, Writing

I

15   New World Dreams
17   Miss Killough
20   First Night in the Tropics
22   Leona
23   The Find
25   Last Night in the Tropics
27   Voices: Four Meditations and a Lament
30   Letter from the Desert
31   Jungle Lover: A Letter
33   For Big Tree
34   A Horse in the House

II

36   In the Botanics: Edinburgh
37   Snowdrops: Edinburgh
38   Snowdrops: Glasgow
40   Wedding Story
42   The Loch
44   Barn Dance
46   The Holly Thief
48   Birchwood in Fife
50   Night-Night
52   The Bathroom: Midnight
54   Homers
56   The River
58   Chinese
60   Red Letter Day
64   Animal
66   A Brief History of Your Breasts
68   Jenny in July

III

70 Alberta Morning
72 Buffalo
74 Hazards
76 Grace
78 O Canada
80 Japanese
82 Visiting Birder
84 The Hunt
92 Spring on the Prairies
94 The Father

Anyone who observes what is going on around us with a certain degree of detachment must admit that the world is being buffeted by despair and a mysterious, inexplicable love.

EUGENIO MONTALE

Loving, Writing

If your love was true
and you lose it, what have you lost?
Not the act of loving. That's yours.

If your words were true
and you lose them, what have you lost?
Not the act of writing. That's yours too.

In loving, in writing, how can you
hold onto a finished thing? Whether
you lose it or put it beneath glass,

it is the act itself you must cherish.
For what's left when the moment has passed,
the wind will carry. Despite you.

I

New World Dreams

'... deep surroundin' darkness
Is aye the price o' licht.'

HUGH MacDIARMID

I

Arrived safely. But already too late.
I rummage through bottomless chests of maps,
straighten the bleeding crucifix, make up
tales to fit the tapestries. A cool room
with an arched veranda's been prepared...
Sun burns through honeyed stone; the moveless air
never clears its hot reek of burning flesh
and native women. Their dark eyes hate us
or they die. (There is a novel in me;
its pages weigh me down like coffin lead.)
I stare over harbour and sparkling sea.
I spin the globe. Find Eldorado, I say.
Drive on! Find the counterweight to balance
all this suffering, boredom and death.

II

Out of deep surrounding darkness, a globe
of Borgesian exactitude. It glows,
though parts of its surface are dark-edged, furred
with jostling moths. *Lacrimae addicta.*
Throughout the dry seasons of history
they have swept through the forests and savannahs
of Africa, Asia, America...
Fastening on the most placid creatures
or the most weak, they worry the eyeball
then gorge on the salt-licks of their tears.
No one's ever starved feeding on suffering,
sadness and pain. Spin the globe. See! Rainbows
arch over the giant cataracts
they have made. Bright blue butterflies dance there.

III

Take a hammer to the night. Rake over
the glittering shards. The stage-set plaza
with its crumbling delicacy, violence
throbbing down the alleys. From dark doorways
the calls: 'Good marijuana, good mari...'
'Eh gringo! Wan' fuck you over the moon.'
('Careful mister, these people not your friends.')
In a café so open it hovers
in the velvet air, a lusty negra
thrusts the pink throttle of her tongue at me:
it has wings like a bird or the flowers
one feeds on. Fear and desire: these you must pass
to the lone singer's resigned, happy songs.
'We are here,' one song says. 'We are here.'

IV

What once lived here lives on in the outskirts,
the hot outback. ('They'll skin you alive,
mister' – crimson your face with chicken blood.)
Stay with the church, the bars and the music.
Let the golden beer cool you and the hawkers
move among you: nuts, roses, a statuette
of a saint. And more insistently
the beggars: the rheumy-eyed kids, the youth
hauling his eloquent stumps through the dirt,
the hopelessness of the old. Eat and drink.
This is the world. Rest assured, this is the world.
Before it slips from your grasp with its ghosts,
choose. It is our privilege and mild pain
to bless dead eyes with arbitrary coins.

Miss Killough

(source: one of Elizabeth Bishop's letters)

Old friends know best
to give me space. Take Lota, my old school chum,
content to leave me for hours soaking
in this deep bath, listening
to Dona Elizabetchy's old Corona
clacking away like an angry remonstrance.
Though the poems of hers I've seen are perfect,
clear as water, the clack clack clack
of these sharp black tongues
takes me back
to the operatic rows
between mama and Miss Killough.
For days they'd build up, mama muttering
under her breath at Miss Killough's
coolly appraising eye, becoming ever more
agitated till she was tented
in silence as the thunder brewed.
The smallest incident triggered the storm:
Miss Killough pointing out, 'Senhora,
it does the girls no good to see you
snacking so.' Or, 'Well Senhora,
even though it is carnival I think
in this you go too far.'

And I see them before me
still trapped in the languages
which made them, mama's arms flayling
with her tongue, 'O Sacco de Jesus!
a thousand curses on me – but...' as she stamps
round the room lifting and laying books, letters,
trinkets; Miss Killough simply growing taller,
whiter, more thin-lipped. 'Well, Senhora,
I'm sure I've no wish to stay
where I'm not wanted.' And in the silence
which follows, the creak of her steamer trunk
and the dull thwacks of heavy underwear
are the loudest sounds in Rio.

Still as a candle, mama now holds
the centre of the room, flickering at us
with her pale flame of a face. First
at my sister then at me. 'Maria Cecilia,
what do I do with such a woman?' I shrug
hopelessly. 'Then so be it!
Let her go back to her precious Aberdeen.'
But we both know mama will soon
be knocking on Miss Killough's door
and begging a pardon Miss Killough
will readily give. For in truth what has she
to go back to? By all accounts a cold grey city
that stinks of fish – though she always
talks of it fondly, always says
she'll never get used to this heat.

Next morning as if nothing had happened
we'd have a bowl of oatmeal
(as I still do) and set off for our daily walk.
The Botanical Gardens, early,
were her favourite: royal palms
and hummingbirds. Rarely the beach.
'A lady should be pale,' Miss Killough
used to say. 'I want no part in raising
bothy quines.' But she smiled in saying it.
I still carry her picture
in my prayer book looking as I imagine
a Scotch Highlander does – thick with tweeds
and with a firm expression that says,
'Maria Cecilia, I know what's best for you.'

At forty-five I'm still regarded
as something of a beauty in this city
of beautiful women: smooth skin, perfect teeth,
a blond mane and for interest's sake,
as Miss Killough used to say, one brown eye
and one blue, bright as a hummingbird
in the dark. A thoroughbred
I move through the city's moneyed heart
as keen a student as any of the hierarchies
of blood our history's composed of. Yet
fifteen years after her death, I hear

her Rs like waves rolling through my speech
and find myself turning
from those English salon ladies who spurned her;
or saying to my patriotic hosts, 'Oh
this hopeless country! It's a wonder
anything gets done.'

To her hopeless charges
she left all her little money, even took
to their religion just before she died.
She said her own church seemed cold to her;
in her last days she wanted something more friendly
than bare stone walls. 'Maria,' she said
at the end, 'it's a bonnie name.'

None of us had seen her
softening. How could the edges
of her hard country blur with ours?
Or more remarkably Scotland's grey charms
enter our souls. But I carry
her exile within me as well as
the aches and pains of deportment I try
to soak away. So I have one blue eye
on Rio, the other – the brown –
on Scotland's flinty shores.
In Nossa Senhora da Candelaria
I light a candle for her
whenever I can. I always look
at the painting of Antonio de Palma surviving
the shipwreck, but it's Miss Killough
I see raising her skirts
to climb ashore.

First Night in the Tropics

The sun bronzed
the palm-fronds
and disappeared.
Took with it
everything. Even
snuffed the egrets
that rode like tall
white candles
on the cattle's altar-
backs. The road
came to mean
kerosene lamps
and someone rocking
in a roadside shack;
figures walking
that were darkness
thickening, that night
snatched back
again. The path
was 'Cuidado, boys!
Cuidado!' Roots.
Rocks. Water.
Was a false trail
of fireflies –
now here!
now there! –
in the thick maze
of air. And that night,
past the neat
village that slept
in its hollow beneath
the salt-spilled sky,
I caught sight of
the bright green
sliver of a lizard
shinning up a wall –
a watchstrap
with no watch

and no need; for the time-
less days stretched out
there, in the long darkness,
ready to match
my vision of them –
a long string
of precious stones
being polished
by the pounding sea.
I saw a perfect
breathless
crescent of sand,
(it was! it was!)
a fringe of dense
coconut palms,
leaning towards
limpid, blue light;
and every piece
of flotsam waited –
even as warm rain
in a single sheet
drove down – to sing
like a crickets' chorus:
    Make me
    into a cup, a pestle,
    a fruit bowl...
    Why not
    live here
    always?

Leona

Leona, the wisdom of the village,
sits on her haunches on the new-swept earth
before a heap of plantain. Fried they will make
that night's only meal. She skims a large knife
under the green peel, then cuts the white flesh
in half and drops it in a cracked, blue basin.
Now and again she stops to brush her brow
with the back of her hand: elegant, assured.
Her husband is out of work. *Trabajo?*
There's none around here. I hear him playing
with a toddler-child inside their wooden
kitchen-shack. And hear the overloud clacks
of the domino players, chap-chapping
in the strained light beneath the lemon tree.
The same ones yesterday, today, tomorrow.

Over in the tiny village store, rich
with the clammy smells of coconut and rum,
a sixteen year old mother turns her chair
from the orange glow of the kerosene lamp
to suckle her baby in the half dark.
Half interested, a young brother looks on.
Añiano serves everyone in rota,
one item at a time. Unschooled, he scrubs
his calculator of its thin web
of numbers and tries again. At the last
he turns its bland face to the customer
in apology for what *it* has done.

Leona has determined her eldest
of four will not get pregnant at sixteen.
No *novios* for Juliana yet.
At seven each morning she must put on
a plain, blue blouse and take the truck to school
with the other girls. But each afternoon
she has English lessons down on the beach,
choosing the scantiest of chic dresses
from a glossy, coloured catalogue.

The Find

'Are there Spaniards in heaven? Then light the fire.'

ENRIQUILLO: TAINO FREEDOM FIGHTER

After the great storms
which dyed the sea dark red
and left the piled coconuts
like a massacre of bearded skulls
along the beach, there is
a calmness in the village tonight –
a fresh space, which is open
to possibility. As if to match
something to the moment,
Cañete produces
a small brown object
and offers it in the palm
of his hand. It is a perfect
Taino axehead of dark
obsidian stone. He has found it
in the forest. 'This is what happens
when lightning strikes stone.'
'Yes,' says another,
'I've seen it happen.'
We pass the stone
around our huddle, feeling
its cool smoothness
in our hands.
          As we look,
the group is joined
by a young man, who is soon
nodding agreement. 'Once
I saw a horse struck
by lightning,' he tells us.
'It just stopped
dead in its tracks.
I went up to it
and touched it
on its forehead.

Like this…' Delicately,
his fingers anoint
the silence.
'It collapsed
into a pile
of white ashes – right there
in the middle of the road.'

*

Yet not for long.
Soon it is back;
but this time, it is a horse
made from ashes
which stands before you
in the middle of the forest path,
as the sun makes the earth
steam around its grey,
ghostly legs. Go on,
touch it. It is yours now,
is it not? Touch it:
it will collapse again
and be nothing.
Yet how sure
seems its body
on its four pillars
of ash. It stands
in your mind more rootedly
than the lightning which killed it
or the storm of fires
in which Enriquillo
finally drowned.

Last Night in the Tropics

On the dark veranda
I swing on a hammock,
my feet at the Pleiades,
a cool beer knocking
against a naked thigh;
the best this side
of Paradise. I try
to sum up, to the sound
of cicadas' dull clicks,
time's precious gifts
to me. Not days
like the faulty tap's drip...
drip... as if each sun rose
with a numbered core
and at its dying glow
could be stoppered and stored;
nor days so rich
in memory, slippy
and various as fish,
whole journals aren't nippy
enough to catch them.
Once I'd thought time here
was space. I saw a room
burning with a clear,
blue light, a room in which
each event – the sighting
of whales, a good rich
meal, the plunging flight
of pelican, the weight
of tropical rain – each
could be located
in its proper place.
In this clear bay, time's laws
(to me) seemed all at sea.
But then at last I saw
a clear chronology,
an order that rang true;
and the order was
one day all through,

from roots to shaws,
perfectly remembered.

So I lie here,
where I saw a herd
of whales' tails clear
the sparkling waters
(how long ago?),
a large pink blotter
soaking the last glow
from my perfect day.
I slug the warming beer
and from nowhere, suddenly
a bat flops against me,
the briefest fright
for both of us.
I trace its flight
back to the deepest crush
of blue-blackness. Smells
of ginger and garlic
drift round the wall
from where light licks
into the darkness.
The split ends of easy
conversation – a mesh
of 'Pass me please...'
and 'All I really miss...'
drift my way too.
It will be like this
when I am gone. Soon.
The same ease; the same
stars curled around
this rich and open home.
The ghostly plantain,
the cut-out palm,
share my conspiracy,
for suddenly I am gone;
part moon, part stars and sea:
the bright fireflies that zoom
from palm to palm
are part of the atoms
of delight that I am.

Voices: Four Meditations and a Lament
(on words scratched on the windows of Croick Church in Ross-shire)

1 *Glencal peopl was in the churchyard here*

From Maeshowe to Pompey; from Lascaux to Tobruk:
the ancient mark of momentary presence,
the signature of ghosts. With their absence they paid
for this gaunt landscape, those who sought shelter
in the churchyard, too pious to enter the church itself.
Lit by small fires in the damp, tented graveyard,
the peat-cutting hand cut into the glass. He signed
in another tongue to reach another shore:
they had been broken on their own, their name a song
already fading. I can still catch his breath
as fist and flint loop across the small diamond pane.
This is harder than breaking rocks! But it must be said.

2 *Murder was in the year 1845*

Call a spade a spade. There are many ways to skin
a rabbit and none knew more of them than they did.
First you must kill it. Deal in facts as the graveyard does:
birth, death – murder. This voice is the bitter whisper
in the wind: you can't shake it this end of the glen.
Though the murder written of here didn't happen here,
as the lament that sings in Wounded Knee was composed
many years before it, and the murder of Kurds
driven like deer was in someone's eyes long before it.
Savages all, bent over greenwood fires, despair
a field creature hiding in the dark litter of their eyes.
The Lord is our shepherd but let the year not forget us –
each numeral painfully scored into the singing winds.

3 *Glencalvie people the wicked generation*

As if they were another species, someone
from *The Times* spoke for them to the wider world,
told of the wretched spectacle they'd made leaving
their land at last, refugees with carts of children,
the poor supporting the helpless poor. Anon wrote:
If such as happened here transpired in the south
there would be outrage. (His pen; their flint.) But they
being damned, damned themselves. Though they grew like rowans
in the rock of the land, their spirits cracked
like firs without it. This voice is the saddest fiction
and they took it to the grave. The wretched of the earth –
shaking the journalist's hand, he thought, like children.

4 *Glencalvie is a wilders...*

Passing over a swell of lonely hills that sap
the earlier green of the strath, black cloud shadows
like lids in the sky, close on clear runs of sunlight.
The rubble of an ancient broch can give no shelter here,
nor the ruined sheepfolds pinned to the hills.
The faint light still catches the last of their voices
muted by horse chestnut, sycamore and ash,
though the wind soughing through the tall spruce bites
back the last word. Their backs turn from you now, their carts
move off and they fade, leaving not the pristine world
of *Walden*, but a hard land that once gave shelter
turned into a land of ghosts, a wilders...

CODA: *Lament*

It is above all and beyond all doubt a doleful song,
characterised by a melismatic note, a monotonous tone,
appearing to involve a repetitive attempt
at a drone-like narration of some overwhelmingly sad and
                                               disturbing events
which seem to have affected the home.

The singer's inner agitation is clearly shown
in the way his face appears drained and drawn,
with a fixed smile as ironic accompaniment
        for such a doleful song.

One is left with the lasting impression
of a man who has been battling with tears too long;
but who, even in exhaustion, cannot cease his lament.
His is the haunting voice of peoples whose futures are rent,
whose stolen past cannot come again.
        It is above all a doleful song.

*(From the observations of a musicologist on an untranslated song by
an Aché Indian whose tribe faces systematic genocide in Paraguay.)*

Letter from the Desert
(Nazca, Peru)

Today we drove deep into the dry heart
of a real red desert. Three of us, miles
from anywhere in an acre of graves.

Have I told you before that I miss your smile?

We moved silently among the unmarked
anonymous dead, past the graves of those
who'd lain centuries uncared for, unmourned.

I thought of light through tree-lined avenues.

The heat of the desert sun preserved them:
shallow craters dug for the hereafter,
long robbed of all but white bones and powdered sand.

I listened to the wind for your laughter.

Some sat huddled like the sad family groups
I've seen here camping on the streets;
but most lay, long free of their rotting bonds.

Soon the chestnuts will burst out in green sheets.

The brown mummified paw of a small child
was pointed out to us, and a broad weave
of hair the length of a full-grown man

and a whole new world breathe with fresh, green leaves.

He let the wind carry it; a banner
for all their dead. Then he brought his hand down
and the hair lay across four smooth, white skulls.

Have I told you before that I miss your smile?

And all that is known about these people
is learnt in such places. They left no songs
but the wind passing over their bones.

But the wind passing over their bones.

Jungle Lover: A Letter

Today I walked deep into the humid heart
of a real, green jungle. And yes, you would
believe it, got lost. Though the fading sun

still played on the high canopy, for me
down below it was already too late.
At the slow, brown-bellied river I found

my first dead end. By then the crude map
was a pale glow in my hands. I'd as well
read the broad, black leaves on the forest floor.

I didn't panic straight away. A lightening
of foliage gave – disappointingly early
I thought – some prospect of success.

But it was only a gash of sunlight
through a treefall the hungry canopy
had not yet closed over. The path led back

into the dark tunnel and I'll admit,
yes, to my first real twinge of panic then.
I start to jog along the faint, grey light

of the wrong trail. I call out but the dense
foliage absorbs every sound I make
and returns silence. Deafening silence.

Vicious thorns snag me, roots trip me, tree trunks
slam into me. I stumble off the path
into closed darkness. Lost. Utterly lost.

Covered with sweat and insect repellent
(my one foresight) I wait, feeling strangely
calm now I know my efforts are hopeless.

One more black silhouette in the jungle,
I threaten nothing but sit on my branch,
attentive as all the creatures must be

which hoot, whistle and breathe in the stillness.
And slowly the forest reveals itself:
the cry of a bird, the crash of a branch,

the rustle of leaves as a small creature
moves through the forest litter. I too turn
nocturnal, one with the living darkness:

let daylight find me. And find this letter too.
It will tell you of torchlit seekers
who never reach me, though we circle each other

like jaguars along the clotted paths.
At times I think I see the candlelights
of a lodge within reach – the warmth of food

and laughter, the tame macaw I wrote you of
that tried to crack my fingernails apart.
But some choice makes me snuff all of them out

to head back into this mapless green world
where I can feel closer to your heartbeat.
And everywhere I go the forest follows

flowing into my traces like the sea
into empty scoops of sand. Between the lines
of this letter, listen for the broken sounds

as one more ageless tree tires, falls and drowns.

For Big Tree

(Big Tree is a strangler fig.)

I walk the forest floor and rarely look up
from the light-hungry leaves, the fallen trees
rich with the fast-forward of tropical
decay, the militant lives of the ants.
But then I arrive at the great winged roots
of Big Tree and their slow, gentle curves say
Follow – into the smooth, thick trunk and up
to where the silver arteries are spread
with profit over the thick canopy.
Below, I stand in the deep, mossy shade
while up there small green arrows drink the last
sunlight. But Big Tree – tallest and proudest
in this forest – is not a tree at all.
Listen to its story.
                    A thumbnail seed
lands high on the trunk of a lapuna.
The wind takes it there or a choosy bird
wipes it from its beak. The seed germinates
and sends missionary roots to the thin
earth for nourishment. These roots grow. Do you
believe how these roots have grown? Now they flare
out into giant flanges to buttress
the new tree, enfolding the lapuna
which slowly withers within its casing.
But this new tree, this freak, dependent plant,
has not finished yet. Now it reaches high
above the lapuna's old crown. It clears
the dense, green canopy and emerges
into an infinity of blue light.

I like to stand by Big Tree between two
cool, hollow wings. Big tree, *mi madre*,
I feel the sure spread of your roots. I feel
the good sunlight drunk deep within you.
I find it comforting to know what first
appeared as misfortune, time and effort
has transformed; that an old host, having played
its part, decays in favour of a fresh,
green self, rooted in water and sunlight.

A Horse in the House
(translated from the Spanish of Wáshington Delgado)

I keep a horse in my house.
During the day it stamps the floor
beside the kitchen.
At night it sleeps at the foot of my bed.
With its horseshit and its neighing
it makes life inconvenient
in a small house.
But what else can I do
while I journey towards death
in a world on the edge of the abyss?
What else but keep this horse
like a pale shadow of the open prairies
beneath the open air?
In the city – dead, anonymous –
among the nameless dead, I walk
like one death more.
People look at me or don't look at me,
stumble into me and excuse themselves
or curse me: they don't know
I keep a horse in my house.
In the night, I caress his mane
and give him a lump of sugar
just like in the pictures.
He looks at me blandly; some tears
appear about to fall from his round eyes.
It's the fumes from the kitchen or sometimes
the despair of living in a patio
of twenty square metres
or sleeping in a bedroom
with a floor of wood.
At times I think
I ought to let him go free
to search for his own death.
But what of the distant prairies
without which I could not live?
I keep a horse in my house
desperately bound
to my dream of liberty.

II

In the Botanics: Edinburgh

An hour till dusk. The castle lodges its span
in the crook of a giant sycamore.
Through arteries of beech, the domes and spires
of the city turn to a scattered fan
of embers. I kick chestnuts from the path
and, like a bird scuttering through the black
skirts of a rhododendron, forage back
into my past. That's when your airy laugh
calls me. Maria Angeles Huarte,
your daughters share spirits with the squirrels
they feed, dancing between silver birch light.
You yourself know the moment's poetry:
'See!' the sooty heron's labouring flight,
the cyprus where its wings stumble and curl.

Snowdrops: Edinburgh

'Come now,' my grandpa said, 'none of your nonsense.
Out with it.' My school reading of *A Man's*
A Man my mother thought was so intense.
Grandpa sipped tea from a saucer as he listened.
I sensed my mother's discomfort for us both.

Near death he sent home his gold watch for me.
On one side of a baroque gold fob a frisky cock
mounts a hen etched into an oval stone block
the colour of semen. It took years to pluck them free,
those white heads squawking in the undergrowth.

Snowdrops: Glasgow

Today, don't ask how,
but as if in a dream
I found myself washed up
on the city's Green

where, by statute, a grid
of iron clothes poles
remain – social archaeology
neither buried nor hid

in the nearby glass museum.
On a good drying day
like today, they trap
the sun's rays

like the light hair
on a girl's arm, the saplings
of a well-thinned forest.
And there I took my rest

running my hands
over their cool bulbous tops,
seeing white sheets (soft
white, wash-day hands)

bellying and writhing
in the breeze. And I
was overcome by a tide
of elation, unbidden

as its dark opposite,
as I turned in and out
those dusty poles –
my heart, a shout –

feeling the dissipation
of my love as it flowed
from me, an aimless
felicitation

for the hard earth.
And where it fell,
it was like the snowdrops
that, spreading all

through the woods,
give such lift to the moods
of those seeking the Spring
in themselves.

Wedding Story

...then, as we approach
an empty cottage, whose
rusted gate's spreadeagled
against a mossed-grey dyke,

the ghosts of all creatures
that have lived there take flight.
A great wheel of energy
suddenly shoots to life,

a breath too fast for sight,
till the autumn sun blunts
each spoke into a fist
of light. For a moment

something in us answers,
something more than the shout
it's so simply dressed in;
but soon it too is lost

in the lucid air.
The last pigeon flusters
up from silvered rafters,
dissolves through a skylight

the breadth of the roof
and we are left to walk
the two small rooms alone.
A web of small duties

enfolds me as we pass,
crossing the nettled floor,
and I feel again that warm
disturbance to my thoughts

you have lately become.
Below the cottage, we crawl
into the daguerreo-
type darkness of a crypt

of hawthorns. Their dead leaves
are just turning to mulch.
Here, from a broken stem
down the slope, branching out

over the whole damp floor
is a graveyard of empties,
a glass obsolescence
arrested in full flight.

Like scavengers, we move
among the twisted pillars,
picking up a jar, squat
and fat, that triggers

memory, a brand name
long-swallowed. Some still bear
the ghostly scuffs of – what?
Others make folds of moss,

bottle-shaped. We try
their weight in our hands,
like old thoughts or words
whose meaning had once been clear;

then toss each gently back
into its open grave;
their muted vowel-sounds
hanging in the fusty air.

Soon now we shall find
the Roman road which leads
to the sea. We'll know it
by the powdery earth

scutted by the warren,
by the crow buffeted
sideways. We'll take it
with the milk churn ringing.

The Loch

I've found that loch again – the one
where I stand at autumn's edge
and look over a broken stretch
of tussocky grass, a handful
of young birch trees; and imagine

a clear sandy edge of water
before depth is lost to tangled
black weed, rhythms of stirred up silt.
Something breaks in the pine forest
beyond it – a dead branch? Or deer?

Two or three, moving down through firs
which darken to blue in the late
afternoon light: deer drawn down
through sweet-smelling pines, their hooves light
on the pine floor; deer drawn down to water.

A bird call fills the clearing then,
spreads out from its watery core.
Nothing else. I've never been here
before, so can't comprehend how
something quite so still, so complete –

ly of the moment, can carry
so many other lochs within.
Yesterday's art gallery held
another kind of stillness. Keen,
attentive as deer, people picked

their way between exhibits; each
pausing wherever they were drawn.
One man clapped a child to his chest
to share his vision: Goncharova's
Soldier in the Forest, Chagall's

The Poet Asleep. At each green dream,
he ruffled the hair of the child
with his lips, so that it stood up
there like a tuft of bog cotton.
Just before the evening chill breaks

my concentration, I feel lips
gently brush the base of my skull.
Somehow I have always felt loved.
Nothing says that in the picture
but it's there. In the darkness

firs rise from the nape of the loch,
the black roots of gathered up hair.
An early star burns needle sharp
at the forest's edge. With each light step
a bruised scent of pine fills the air.

Barn Dance

(in the Central Belt)

Horsey, horsey, don't you stop,
just let your hooves go clippety clop.

We take the mnemonic, but leave the dance,
the barn's store of stoorie warmth,
its whoops and giddy laughter.

'Want to see the calves?' Across
the muddy, moonlit yard is a shadow
the shape of a hangar.

Two calves rise from darkness there,
uncross themselves and straightleg it
to our still, cupped hands.

Once I taught calves to drink,
letting them suckle my fingers
in a bucket of milk. And now

you too will feel the light, damp
clamp of a mouth, the smooth bridges
of teeth, as one tawny calf

and one brown draw in everything
that inhabits this cool spacy air –
all but our awareness

of their sexual slurp. We sense,
more than see, our eyes smile. 'Tickles,
doesn't it?' 'Yes (a laugh) yes.'

I run my hand along the soft,
curved ridge of my brown's neck,
petting it. Oh, my city roots!

Down the lane, at the second bend,
where the music dies and the beaded lights
of an estate have us surrounded,

44

we nuzzle each other in the silence,
in the middle of this dark green lung.
Horsey, horsey, don't you stop!

We turn our hands, sniffing
our fingers, like the first people.
The milk of children is on them.

The Holly Thief

A week till Christmas and treeless.
All those spewing from the shop doors
would bulk us out. Still, you're let down.

A sprig of holly on my desk,
full of good cheer, winks at me. So
when it's dark I take secateurs

and slip out to the ill-lit street.
The gunpowdery smelling cold
has cleared them. Now enter the thief.

The tree grows behind the glass-
topped wall of the petrified house
where no one's ever seen. Its mass,

black in the darkness, overhangs
the pavement; its gloomy eaves pour
shadows down the wall. The branch-tips

come within my reach. I want ones
gifted with berries; each a bright
scarlet maraca, soundlessly

shaken as I tug down a branch
by a leaf, then a twig, then twist
the secateurs' claw till it gives –

sshh! Only waves of hooks hold it.
Too poor a berry harvest there,
I'm back up on tiptoe again

burying my wrists in the thick
of the crop. I'm catching on now:
waiting, watching for the full beam

from a car to turn up the road.
There are two images then. One,
the yellow light cascading through

the dark green vaulting of holly,
firing scattered clumps of berries.
The other, a thief on tiptoe

reaching up at the top road bend
into a blind galaxy, heavy
as earth; only when you have passed

pulling out yet another branch
to be part of the Christmas bush
of the first year of his marriage.

Birchwood in Fife

We skirt the animal swell of the birks
as they head for the sea – their dark outline's
as sharp as the coast's. At the shore you find
a loose wicket gate where a small stream forks
and seeps away into merse and rocks.
Along the tree-lit path I slot the blind
heel of my hand between the simple round
meetings of branches; and up the smooth bark
maps I count diminishing torsos.
Each one glows with a livelier light
till deltas of twigs where scribbled against
the clear blue sky is the flying circus
of a rookery. Back down to earth,
expecting a plosive springtime thunder,
you seize my hand in yours and implore
'Can't you feel a thing? Come on, yourself.'
The baby's tucked in its toes or somer-
saulted away: my spatulate fingers
are all thumbs. In the bath too you'll stare
down on yourself as though your core
shines through the ivory drum of your skin.
'Did you see that? Did you see that?' The moment's
passed and with it your disappointment.

In a deep still pool we peer in vain
for shadows of trout to shadow-shine; then,
a smoke of rain a sprint from us, seek shelter
under dense rhododendron. The air's
rich with wild garlic; and field gentian,
in a scatter of deep blue shocks, becalm
all that surrounds them. Time now to leave
this place where all seems inwardness and love;
to set off back to our ill-fitting home.
At the edge of the woods, through sycamore
light branches and buds, we watch as a crow,
rising from the great tilled prose of the soil,
jacks itself into the almost-sky then veers

off on a mission. Soon those tight brown fists
will unfold into the expectant air
their green palms. Magic. I part your damp hair –
in the cleared copse of your neck plant a kiss.

Night-Night

You take to bed early
these days. When I join you
you're already well away, face crushed
to the edge of the bed;
a great white booby bird
sniffing the muddy currents
from the wreck of papers,
slippers, hairdryer, books
etc below your beak.
Or lying like a cartoon
character just as sleep
has ambushed you, open
pregnancy book tilting
from your fallen knees. (So
how many times have you read
that section on 'vomit'?)
Standing in the middle
of the room tonight, you
lift up your nightdress. 'Look,
they're getting bigger now' –
your breasts, growing like fruit,
marbled with thin blue veins –
the faintest hyacinth
tracery. I take their weight
on my hands and hold them
while you float on my tide
in the lamplight, the trees'
sloe-black hearts behind you.
Once upstairs you lead me
again though the keyhole
patterns of growth. 'And now
it's this size,' holding up
a pinky. I recall
among grey filings that
electric energy,
one Escher I can't lose
the sense of: a seed-sized

heart pumping as the legs
like fusewire lit from within
knitted furiously.

I'm not ready for sleep.
On the TV, tracers
stitch up the night sky
over lunar deserts;
men offer lives like crumbs
on their fingertips, eyes
expecting no mercy.
Here, the barnacles honk
as their slow Vs pass us;
large, loose snowflakes launch
themselves at the window,
the wind giving their flight
a final tick. They land
with a touching lightness.
Whatever connects them
is lost in the darkness.

The Bathroom: Midnight

Not to waken you, I leave all lights off
to squat down amid the darker shadows
of all that in this shifting time we've brought
here: baskets, lamps, a fifties radio...

Like those washed-out landscapes you drive past, fast
in the night or mist-drenched day: milky heads
of trees, the swell of buildings lying vast
distances over frosted fields, till the road

twists and farmhouse lights rush towards you.
Resting on chalky thighs, I try the weight
of what's to come beyond the faint grey-blue
edged trees, but taste only air and light.

And as air grows thinner and light darker,
death becomes as clear as the cormorant
frozen at the weir, its spread wings blacker
than itself. My frail mother takes my hand:

'You are the sixth in line to bear your name.
Some day the grandfather clock will be yours.'
It anchored the bright galaxy of home –
once thought fixed – whose fractured light pours

over us. At its rim I can make out
the shining bone-white speck of an eggcup;
one of those still-life details by Van Eyck
that draws you close to the canvas to probe

how the eye can be convinced by a few
deft strokes of oil. But the eggcup remains
real in its realm as this basket with its (now)
waxen glow whose roughness will come with dawn.

For in the simple dawn all will be revealed:
the curve of the lamp, the chunky brown knobs
of the radio. Light will put the seal
on the whole Vuillard crush and objects mob

us like seagulls from their cramped surfaces
in their desire to be loved. We have made
our inheritance too, have made our place
from others' places. But connections fade

and sometime, my child, this jerry-built wing
will seem all for you. May you love it in all
its particularity – nothing wrong
with that – yet sitting in this crowded stall,

I think a landscape that also rings true
is the early one that looked so fragile
and washed-out. The one as children we rush through,
bursting through fields for mile upon mile

until up ahead with a welcoming glow
we see farmhouse lights shining on fresh snow.

Homers

The farmer's son in Kintyre
gave us four pigeons
at our holiday's end – two each
and we could choose, though not
the most dependable homers.

He scooped them from the rafters
of the outhouse above
the grey drills of shit. It took
two hands to hold one; one to lock
round its tail and feet

as the other calmed it,
calmed myself, running a finger
round the thick thumb
of its head, over a nutmeg-
speckled breast.

Home in Edinburgh
our neighbour had no problem
holding my two birds, one cooped
in each large fist. Poor homers –
lazy, unlucky or what? –

while I idled in the cool hut
waiting their coffin-lid
scratchings, he'd plucked them, feet
like roots, from his lime-green
rows of seedlings.

Voyagers, I'd thought them
and launched them from open palms
to gain blue and in great arcs to skim
some imagined geography
home. Tonight

the pigeons' heads poke
from our long-dead neighbour's fists
as tiny wavering flames
against the long shadow
of the hedge. We fly

always above open palms
and nothing brings us home.
It was weeks before I trusted
those pigeons again. And when I did
they were gone.

The River
(from a photograph by Robert Capa: China 1938)

Thunder cracks, rolls
off the mountains; the valley fields
are lit by lightning. In the storm light
distant birds turn to white constellations
promising change. I sit in my room,
barely touch the plate of fish and rice
the old woman brings, shuffling in nervously,
a clutch of children under her greasy skirts.
In the courtyard, ragged hens hide under the eaves
as hailstones the size of berries drive down
onto thatched roofs; all night waterfalls of rain
pour from gutters which cannot hold them.

This morning children wake me,
giggling as they crunch though hailstones
steaming in the soft sun. The air feels pure again,
light again, the sky blue, as if all that violence
was to give us this one clarified day.
Now the river's swollen, crept right up
the banking; its surface plated
as rhinoskin, swirling, eddying,
a current even the oarsman can't predict –
and he's been reading this stretch of river
all his working life. To him the river's
adversary enough; he looks no further
than it, bracing himself to hold
the huge oar steady as the current threatens
to bear us all away. He whoops and shouts
through rotting teeth. We don't share
his exhilaration; briefly wonder, Is all this
for the likes of him? I picture his life:
the meagre house with the buckled floor,
his earthy wife, children, pigs and hens.

Last night in his muddy village
an old man told me sixty blue heron
once came to their small pond. Sixty! The sky
was dark with them, as if a river was passing
over your head. When they landed, imagine! –
it was more a forest of heron than a pond.
But these things will happen. Six or sixty.
Six thousand or six hundred thousand.
This is the shore the boatman returns to;
a world of meaningless signs.
My comrades and I are going on;
we have other shores in mind. Already
we carry small wounds: a bandaged wrist,
a plaster beneath an eye – tiny badges of intent.
We crave more. Children they say make the best
killers, and we are little more
than children ourselves, feeling others' lives –
sixty or sixty thousand – brushing past us
like wet grasses on our calves. A good shot,
athletic, light on his feet, leans
towards his target the way we lean
towards this coming shore. And it's not for us
to wonder where such impatience will lead. One
cannot think for so many. Simply let us
be useful. When a freak wind takes
the boatman's broad-brimmed straw hat
and lays it on the river, we watch it
float away, circling in the current –
and would watch it as dispassionately
if the boatman himself were still beneath it.

Chinese

Lying in the bath
    I feel a light breeze
through the skylight
    graze my bare shoulders

and knees. I slip
    down lower and slap
warm water between
    gulches and sluices.

I shut my tired eyes.
    What a night last night!
And the moon Li Po
    would write home about.

From the bridge we watched
    as it rose over
the river and shone
    bright as any shield.

We could have touched it!
    I blink: Liberty's
on the toilet seat
    reaching for the skylight.

A moth's trapped there
    by the wooden frame,
its wings the faintest
    breath. Panic has sapped

its energy, so
    my wife flicks it free
then, panting, shuts off
    the draught from me.

In the final push
    the cord of her robe's
failed her and the globe
    of her stomach's lit

by the sun's last rays.
Li Po lives again
in this final scene.

Pale and dripping wet

he holds the full moon
in his hands at last –
its heartbeat as breath
on his shattered wings.

A Red Letter Day

(headline in the Glasgow Herald: *22 August 1991)*

I

The day you were born was 'A Red Letter Day'.
In the crumbling Empire, the forces of reaction
were sent packing; the Gang of Eight,
after their botched coup, fell on each other
'like cockroaches in a jar'. Stories abounded
of flight and of suicide. Yeltsin
was the hero of the hour: a Russian bear
padding along the terrace of his beseiged White House
or roaring from a tank top: 'The honour and glory
of Russian men-at-arms shall not be stained
with the blood of the people.' Broodily determined
beneath his silver hair, there was yet something cruel
about his lips, something of the thrill and energy
of power in all his movements. While he appeared
as an actor Eisenstein might cast
in some shadowy Russian parable, off-stage
in the Crimea, Gorbachev ordered his own plain
potato face to be videoed, telling it as it was,
as he awaited his diminished return.

Now the tanks which the brave few had rushed
in the fevered television lights with tarpaulins
and wooden beams, whose barrels had sniffed
the air and known it forever changed,
were rolling down Moscow's boulevards
in triumphant retreat. 'The People Have Won!'
'The People Have Won!' Garlands and bouquets
– even numbers for the dead – piled up on the spots
where the three martyrs for freedom
had laid down their lives. Soon
we would all know the looming white faces
of these 'Heroes of the Soviet Union' –
one serious, one smiling, one Jewish.
'Forgive me, your president,' Yeltsin's voice
cracked, 'that I could not protect your sons.'
Already newly-weds visited their shrines

to bless their wedding days; for this was History
and happening so fast, like a great log jam
had broken and the pent up waters
of Freedom and Democracy were rushing
everywhere. With Tsarists shoulder
to shoulder with Anarchists who knew what
the new order would turn out to be.

Sitting alone in the changed world,
my excitement having given way
to a fluid calm, my vision,
even in the fading light, still sharp,
coating each object, as if my looking
conferred light, I cut the headline out.

On 'A Red Letter Day', I watched a surgeon
thrust white hands deep into your mother's stomach,
scrabble about as if there were finishing touches
to be made – a bow to be tied, a feature kneaded
into shape – or as if he were simply gathering up,
this late summer, two handfuls of autumn leaves.
From the gallery I held that feeling
of the leaves holding together between my palms
(a few falling from the edges, but nothing
could break my concentration now) as I raised them
carefully up and up, the blood-smell of autumn
ripening in the air, till with a shout
they were over my head and released
into the wind. Pure joy! A dove
from red silken rags; a head, so
perfect, so beautiful. So it's true, love
can read the writing on the furthest star:
my eyes focussing with the intensity of heart,
body and soul. Then the body in the middle
of this white, this green aquarium light, the body
a warm, a russett, a maple glow. Oh,
I saw you for us both, saw the beautiful boy
rising from his mother's innards, she spread,
spread and used like earth, as like a rose tree,
he seemed to rise by himself through the air,
his pulsing stem the cord rooted
in his mother's earth.

II

Most of the first day all I had of the world
outside were images. On the second I caught up
with the commentators romping around
on their field day: 'In one sense the Soviet Union
may be witnessing the rebirth of the real
revolution rather than a halfway house
through several false ones.' Gorbachev,
another wrote, underlining the point,
'has enabled 1917 to take up
its proper course again where Lenin had led it
astray.' Everyone was a Revisionist now!
Statues of Lenin were toppling, scythed
at the knees: spinning at the end of a crane,
his famous finger pointed drunkenly
from the Baltic to the Black Sea.

'The rebirth of the real revolution' –
imagine it! In a few words – a pen nib
sleighing through the snow – we were moving
back through History, through the whole
'dustbin of history', or at least seventy four years
of blood, bone and gristle. Back through the Years
of Stagnation when lives were simply
stifled, imagination throttled at birth; back
through bare dirty rooms in state mental hospitals,
through gulags of hopelessness, the efficiency
and the lies of Kalinin and Babi Yar
and the millions upon millions
of collective killings: above them the faint
nightingale tongues of Pasternak
and Tsvetayeva; and Mandelstam; and Mayakovsky; in times
when, as Akhmatova told it, 'only the dead
smiled, happy in their peace'. And back again
past the cold white campaigns, the bones
crushed beneath all the strident state monuments.
'Forgive me, your president...' Till at last
arriving at the small village of Vitebsk,
where the innocent Marc Chagall, newly installed
as Commissar for Fine Art, has ordered
posters of giant green cows and flying horses
to float through our imaginations, where lives
his only dream of a perfected world.

'More gas! Gas!' I'd heard your mother shout
and saw her mouth gape like a fish
beneath the mask. Then, surfacing from a dive
down a black rope of pain that seemed to be
crushing the centre of her being, she turned her head
slightly and brushed the midwife's arm
with fingertips to which the blood was just
returning. 'Thank you. You're so kind...'
Nature revealing a truth about her
at that moment as clearly as that day History
had revealed some truth about Yeltsin.
The pain had taken us both by surprise.
'The biggest secret in the world' – so close
to death. 'How long? How long...' Night
became dawn, became day, became afternoon,
as the forces of nature stormed her,
picked her up, dashed her down. Even before
the worst, in a lull, I looked across
her pale, done-in face and exhausted body
to the midwife. 'It does make you wonder
how when there are so many people in the world
and each of them thrust into the world
in such pain, surely enough to know...
enough to value...' 'Forgive me,
your president, that I could not...'

The day you were born, it was
'A Red Letter Day'. Millions of lives...
millions of lives...we've wasted.

Oh my son, your precious, precious head.

Animal

Early morning, the sun
a wheel (if there was one)
on the far horizon
and we in a tall, old
baobab tree, the hot
dung smell of the veldt
rising up to greet us.
In the safe waterhole
below, four buffalo
roll, the gazelles relax
their shivering skins. *Squawk!*
Birrip-pip-pip! Eek-eek
keek-keek! the old ark
settling its timbers
on the blue open sea.

We three are locked into
stillness, the first mumbling
words several lifetimes
away yet. Our son reaches
a warm arm across one
of your breasts to draw milk
from the earthen stack
of your nipple. My head
resting at the soft edge
of his is a smudging
of skins too far: his paw-
plump hand swipes at me
and a sweet tooth of milk
is lost to the fold
of your breast. Still
swipe away! my little one

for I'm firm on this tall
old baobab tree,
happy with this branchline
of evolution. *Squawk!*
Birrip-pip-pip! Lazy
preening, his rinsed blue eyes

between us, a mesh
of arms and thighs, his
finger briefly alighting
on my useless nipple.
So this is innocence,
this measureless moment
when all that concerns us
is the hot shuck of skin
or the casual dismissal
of a fly. But restless
at last he twists between us
and I reach an arm, just,

through the arch of his back
to take him in my arms.
There, gently, I blow and suck,
suck and blow into the soft
creases of his neck.
The animal in him
stills, attentive to the new
as the warmth spreads until
I am taking as well
as giving succour. Breath!
A trick! Kindling of gods,
source of music, stirring
of these lines: breath breaks
our animal spell.
                    Yet
when the bright morning
finally insists
I leave the safety
of this, our crumpled old
baobab tree, it is with
a snort, a loose-
lipped whinny, that naked
I hunt down my clothes.

A Brief History of Your Breasts

They began as seeds
in the darkness and remained so
till conditions were propitious
then exploded
to the size of grapefruit.

Their early history's
anecdotal, virtually
unverifiable, suffice to say
by the time I came to know them
they knew what they wanted.

They'd hang over my face
their heads heavy
as huge orchids, my tongue
the hummingbird that flitted
between them. Making love

we developed an unambiguous
shorthand. 'My breasts,' you'd say,
'Remember my breasts,' as if
I was in danger of flying
or floating off the edge, your breasts

the land to which I must
surely cling. Pregnant
we looked at them lots.
'Look, my breasts,' you'd say
framing them with jersey

or blouse. I noted
in a poem of the time
they were growing like fruit,
'marbled with a thin
hyacinth tracery'. At times

you stepped aside from them
altogether and they hovered
between us like holographs,
though you bore
all their weight. After the birth

they were YOURS and HIS.
Now we discussed them
the most. They were sore,
they were tender, they were full,
they were flooding; tap their tops

some morning, they're
rock hard before he suckles.
We smiled at them now
they'd become so familiar
like a couple of favourite

nieces. Once you even blushed
with pride when I unwittingly
unlocked some of their sweetness
with a serendipitous suck.
                                    Space-time
curved round them

for our son, till eventually
you had to cut him free,
fraying the feeds that bound him,
one by one by one, until
'That's it,' you announced

flapping both breasts
up and down. 'The milk's all
dried up now. Gone.' And that's
as far as we've got in this
brief history of your breasts –

not an elegy but my wonder
in words. For the moment
they are two empty pails
hanging on the door of your chest,
whistling when the wind catches them.

Jenny in July

rolls off the mat, escapes
into the shade of a thicket
of broom. Grass feels

cool on bare arms
and legs, as her hands, still
clumsy as paws, swim

through tall stems, almost
bring heavy seed-heads
to her milky lips. She'll learn.

For now, she's the most
defenceless of all summer's
creatures, abandoned

on a green doorstep
by a father who'd once
dreamed of his daughter

brushed by a fistful
of herbs, rolled in pastry
light as air, cooked

in the wink of an eye.
None of it had bothered
her at all – or him – the dish

was simply a thought –
how tender! how sweet!
Now the yellow stitches

of nipplewort shine
over her, always out of reach,
as she kicks herself ever

further into the world
of flowers and of foxes
along her rich river-bed.

[1994]

III

Alberta Morning

(or How Newness Enters My World)

In the limited, aquatic early morning light,
so loosely shaped by neat suburban fences

and walls, I lose the edge between what's outside
and in. The looming mass of the freezer, the over-

hanging cupboards, the squat presence
of the cooker with its four wide black eyes; each

seems wild, foreign in its own way, as the broad
body of fir framed by the kitchen window,

its branches snout-thick with filaments
of silvered verdigris, seems halfway

to the domesticity of metal. Yet
at its highest fleshy point it's a

timber wolf nosing the striking blue, interceding
between the pure light and the close, dim

interstices of this scene: as the simple pot of cones
you have gathered and placed on the white table

of the deck intercede between the wings
of the fir and barefoot me rooted to this cold floor.

A magpie – one for sorrow – its planed wedge
of a tail perfectly poised, hops across the fading grass,

rhyming with the fence slats. The musty smell
of a full bowl of blueberries beside me billows

into the still air. There is black in the berries.
There is blue in the bird. There is a timber wolf

with blue in the tip of its nose sitting
on top of the fir tree, no not howling, just

staring with my eyes out into the endless blue.
This is how Magritte translates into Albertan

totems; and this is how newness enters my world –
in a simple vocabulary of blue, of fir, of bird

and of berries. Though all along 112th Street
and at all its avenues, the first up look out

on decks and firs and magpies and fences, I hold
this first morning scene – a moment stilled –

as precious, before its power, for me too, is drained
by the commonplace and it is translated

even as the full kettle boils and our child cries,
into the approximations of memory.

Buffalo

The massed aspens rise from the earth
in a seam of black smoke contained
by the gentlest blue; though amongst them

on a path of all the leaves that have fallen
in a week they, and the white spruce too,
are silvered sunlight. I make up breath songs

dance along the track, take in the lake with
first man eyes, the wigeon and teal swimming
in and out among the cat-tails. 'Stop

a moment. Listen.' The last few aspen leaves
on the top branches, withered dry in the sun,
rattle like tokens, wishes in the breeze

'as if a spirit touches only them.'
All else is silence and through the silence,
through the safety of the tall, quivering aspens

we approach a small herd of wood buffalo,
twenty, no more, moving across a clearing
in the forest. A straggling group

of refugees, they push great shoulders,
the weight of shaggy heads through sunlight
as if it were deepest snow. A calf trots

to keep up with its mother, a bull turns
the bevelled anvil of his nose, his black eyes
briefly acknowledge our presence. For the rest

there is only pulling their palettes, leaving
this moment behind. So few! So tame!
Picnicking later in the Indian summer

whose heat stokes up throughout the day, I feel
dampness gather round my collar, my forehead
beads with sweat. So when the rolls of thunder

finally come in the middle of the night
they shouldn't surprise me; yet I sit up
shaken and need to hear you calmly say the word.

That makes two of us who've smelled my fear –
of massed hooves thundering over dry earth
brushing all cover aside. Three, if you count

the lone buffalo who'd stood head on to us
as we parted from the trail. His mussel-
blue tongue, thick as my wrist, plays round his face

before, on legs slim as aspens, he swims
back into the forest's maze, leaving me
threadless, the last leaves trilling above my head.

Hazards

Cradling a bottle of bittersweet
McNally's, feet up, skimming a *noir* thriller,
a sharp-edged seductress on its cover;

with half an eye I take in game two
of the World Series, the Toronto Blue Jays
(one down) versus the Atlanta Braves.

I've given the aerials a good work out,
yet only in the slo-mo of a curving
pitch or in the real time of a sky-kissed

catch is it clear to me what's going on.
A blurred white trail at the foot of the screen
comes between me and my spicy dialogue.

Freezing rain's made road travel hazardous.
Police warn drivers to keep off the roads.
A moment later, the message repeats.

My wife sits where I'd encouraged her to go,
in the warm embrace of a dark theatre
staring towards the bright lights: her head's tipped

back to secure her glasses, her mind's alive,
generous, but framing questions, possibly
for a coffee house later – a café latte

of theatre talk. And all the time
the treacherous world grows more so. Rain welds
into ice where it falls, black roads glint

in moonlight. Cars helplessly collide.
In another room there's another pull.
Our son lies, his plump bottom up in the air,

the soles of his bare feet, two square-
nosed fish on a platter surrounded
by all the softness we want for his world.

I linger over him in the darkness,
edge him on his side and pull the blankets
over the drowsy questionmark he makes:

this, the closest to prayer I get.
We're at the ninth inning when Ed Sprague
takes the ball mid-thigh and devours its heat.

The rest's History. The ball crashes
into an ocean of silenced Braves' fans –
a two run homer, 5 to 4, one game all

and all still to play for. 'I could've crushed
their windpipes one by one and they couldn't
have done a thing to stop me,' sings Easy

also on a roll. *CBC News at Ten*
warns conditions are extremely hazardous
for Croats, Serbs, Bosnians, Somalians,

Tajiks, emigrants, immigrants and Jews.
I sit on the edge of my seat, my beer long
forgotten, waiting for your chopped, cold run

to the door. This is the symmetry of love:
the roots of sympathy growing wider,
deeper, watered by the freezing rains of dread.

Grace

We were the necessary strangers
that Christmas Eve at your parents'
Ukrainian feast. Eyes down, all stood

over the single white candle, a stalk
that burned from a round of plaited bread
as you gave us grace in a language

your childhood tongue never mastered.
Forty-seven, in a loose dress of red red rue,
your mother tactful at your side,

you reached for all the gaping vowels
as a child would, as if your very life
depended on it: *dolia* – fate –

and what fate would you deserve
if you could not save even this short grace
from the oubliettes of history?

So different then from our last goodbyes
when we trailed red prairie dust
in banners all around Two Hills

in search of your summer shack.
In shorts and straw hat, you played,
rather well, the dowager aunt

dismissive of all our excuses
till you bent to blow a smouldering log
to life and soft flakes of blue wood ash

were lost to green poplar tips. Later
we walked to the pond, leaving the vastness
of prairie fields shimmering at our backs.

We were in the landscape now, idling
along its stubbly edges – blowsy poppies,
a darting finch: in some hot agrarian south

of the Old World, closer at last
to the bloodknots of Eastern Europe
you'd spent ten years unravelling.

To fly off the earth (your words) you must
first be standing somewhere: the settled
prairie earth or a darker loam

turned over and over with bones and blood.
There is the gift of bread before us.
As the candle honours and weeps

for it still, you dress the wounds
of an imperfect prayer and send them
like finches, flitting across the abyss.

O Canada

('Below 60' – Whitehorse, Yukon)

In a red-lit space the size
of a small parking lot, seeking refuge
from bright, educated Canadians,
I sit at a bar whose gantry consists
of a huge floodlit case of bottles
of beer and vodka mixers.

'Fuck you, white man!'
Harry calls me over to say,
beading me with brown eyes,
brows gathered beneath his baseball cap.
Then he wants to crush my hand in friendship
before punching an open palm –
'I'm a man but I'm a cat.
Watch it!' A solitary drinker
responds, 'I'm a fuckin Canadian.'
Red, his full, wet mouth not quite
hidden by a grey spade beard, mumbles,
'I'm a survivor.'

The juke-box is doused
for the outcome of the Referendum.
'Harry'll know the results,' says Red,
'cause he's an FBI –
a fuckin big Indian. Now go on Harry,
fuck off… He's one of the best,'
Red tells me, as Harry leaving hold
of our shoulders stumbles off
back to a group of natives pouring over
a globe of silence. 'Yea, never done
a day's work in his life. Not that I know of.'

'Canada's great OK!'
Harry shouts at me across the room.
'Greatest country in the world,' Red nods.
'Why? Cause you can do
what you want. That's why.'

'Fuck Quebec!' the solitary concludes,
encapsulating one view of the night.
He tosses down his short
and slips off his stool. 'I don't give
a fuck!' This of course is the language
of compromise for which Canadians
are renowned over the whole
fucked-up world.

Outside in the crystal cold
I walk the frozen empty streets
feeling that largesse, that bonhomie
given to those who know they walk
the streets of the greatest country
in the world. Back to Hotel Taku –
Taku in the native language, a flight
of geese, and a goose that's cooked that's me;
the only thing stopping me breaking into
    O Flower o Scotland
    When will we see your likes again?
that *Whitehorse Star* headline buzzing
in the back of my mind: 'COYOTES
ARE HUNGRY AND YOUR PET WILL DO.'

Japanese

Husband, allowing
righteous anger
to well up
from he's not sure

exactly where,
for wife's benefit, rips
lettuce leaves from top
of Safeway bag

and hurls them like gloves
to garage ground.
'There!' he says.
'There!' And is off

round block, pluming
breath before him
while booting in
snow piles. Next day

suitably shamed,
'Go on,' he says,
'dearheart, I'll follow,'
and sweeps few

limp leaves
to side, watches
them over time turn
darker, smaller

till they're dried up
old seaweed, simple
washes of ink.
Weeks later

in perilous cold
they get new
lettuce home
already brittle

with frost, all
tiny veins
frozen. 'Beautiful,'
they say, mewing

to each other over open
car boot, each making
moves to cup it,
cradle it inside

to freezer's sensible
warmth. Each defers
one to other, so lucky
lettuce not bleeding

to death. Now
outer leaves lost
for sure. But at least
they will save

the heart. Precious
they bear it together
inside. Neither risks
going anywhere in such

unspeakable cold.
Later husband and wife agree,
mmmm, his dressing tonight
uncannily good.

Visiting Birder

For fifteen minutes, come
December, we'd agreed
to count garden birds.

Snow coated the seeds
of our faulty feeder. Snow
on seeds of snow. Still

chickadees hopped
onto the wooden fence
from the dark folds

of the firtree; blue jays
swooped in from on high.
Then, the cold snap.

Three weeks when
ice packs hit the back
of our throats, our nostrils

cracked like eggs.
With fists of seeds
or crumbs, we tiptoed

at speed into the bell jar
of the deck's cold
concentrate. I threaded

peanuts, hung them
from the roof of the deck.
But no new birds came.

No yellow-bellied
sapsucker, no Bohemian
waxwing or dark-

eyed Junco – none
of the sybillant wonders.
Our two sacks of birdseed

slumped in the cupboard,
the birdbook kept its spring.
The morning of the count

we sat and stared
into the cold white deck,
the dead feeder

domed with snow,
then drifted back
to talk, to the radio.

'Five chickadees,' I
conjured. 'Yes, all counts
're down this year.'

Off phone I sigh
relief. 'But next year,
we can rely on you?'

'Well, sorry but no...'
We'll be back with
Blackbird. Bluetit.

Sparrow. Drenched.
Robin. Crow. Yellow-hammer.
Finch. Come in, come in

you storm-tossed gull.
And, for these few months
of our lives, given

I can slip my head
through customs, five
black-capped

chickadees. Two for joy.
Two for sadness. One
for death.

The Hunt

A final report for Bill Smith (1910-1993).
Iqaluit, formerly Frobisher Bay, Baffin Island: March 1993.

> *'Grief moves from*
> *heart to stapled page*
> *to heart again.'*
> DALE ZIEROTH

I

Through the whisky haze
of dawn, Frobisher's
Arctic gift drifts
along the royal waters

of the Avon; silently
through the bullrushes,
paddle resting
on the kayak top.

A harpoon rises
from a mist of rushes,
a glitter of water
falling from its tip

before it plunges
into a swan's breast
in an outrage of water
and wings.
                    Stillness.

Blood blooming in the water.

From a distance
the virgin queen, whose white
domed forehead's not unlike
a swan's breast, surveys

the chilled faces
which surround her; the soft
cheeks of fish nuzzling the ribs
of a riverbank

as blood billows
over their heads. What she finds
warming in this scene
is its lack of frills:

a swan's neck stretching
in the stubby fist before her;
and an Arctic loneliness
to match her own.

For this, lightly
she traps the damp air
in her ageing hands
again and again.

Of course they rarely hunt like that now, though you can buy tiny
replicas of Inuit in kayaks and other small, rough sculptures of
seals, walrus, narwhal; buy them at the end of a corridor stacked
up with the latest videos. *L.A. Dreams.* Or you can probably buy
them wherever you are, in an elsewhere hungry for what aboriginals
can make: so that much of what's made is made without pride –
for what's a seal to them now? The student holds up earrings for
the teacher.

> – Are they finished? she asks.
> – You tell me, says the teacher.
> – Well I could sell them, the reply.

There's hunger too, always has been, for stories to fill this vast-
ness, to give silence a tongue: stories that beyond the edges end,
for those who look from the boat if not for those from the shore,
most often in disappointment, death: both. Take Henry Hudson,
explorer, cast adrift with his son by the *Discovery*'s put upon crew;
found by Inuit drifting dead in James Bay. Their testimony:

Hudson's son
their first white boy
they tie up
in a dog harness –
for what use can he be? –
and stake outside their tent.
His fingers are already
useless, his fists
paws as he keeps the huskies
at bay
before their noses go down
for the night. And here
the real fight begins
to eke out strength
from a scatter of seal bones
and frozen marrow.
                For tomorrow
blinded by Arctic light,
he pulls for his life
through pack ice green
as apples. His sinews are tough
as a bear's though ridge
upon ridge of ice knives
his bloodied paws. Still
at the day's end
they love him for it,
allow him to nuzzle
their fishy crotches
as once he had his mother's
velvet gown. Now
he's their favourite dog for sure
petted in igloo warmth, loved
back into language,
into the human world
once more. But first
tonight
he must endure
the howls of grief
the doggy whimpers
of a child
at his comfortless fate.

His loneliness is ready
to match it when the big moon
rises over the ice
and he stiffens
to a perfect white.

Sure, the North's more
than stories. But I'm casting around
all the time Bill. This is your trip too
and I'm trying to find a story for you. Here's one
at least to make you smile.

In Inuktitut, Iqaluit means *fish*. But if you spell it beginning I-Q-U
it means *arsehole*. It's not that, yet it still has the portacabin feel of
the place most of which the US Air Force threw up in '42: pro-
visional, sitting on the ice, no purchase on the land – except at
night when the random spray of lights gives it that intimate feel
of places built before the car. An irony to remind you of North
African evenings from the Arctic! And not true of course, though
at times I only recognise roads when skidoos come hurtling down
them. But then they go everywhere, ubiquitous as children on
slides or the giant ravens which croak as if this were a sanctuary
built only for them.

So look around. Where's History?
What constitutes achievement?
Ask Franklin. (Now that
is a good story.)

And once all your stories
have been taken from you...

Who do you fear children?

Drunk men. Dogs.

II

Another three fingers Bill.

We're casting off
heading north again, further
than either of us
has ever been or one
will go again. Could be
we're only making tracks
to silence
          but tell you
what I'm after –

There has to be a poem
after the poem
at last finding
its place in the heart;
not funnelled
into a form as if
its song could be
contained, its grief
assuaged, merely
through its telling.
We'd know then
the grief
on the stapled page
would be a lie
fixed there
out of its true
habitat
where the strong
milky light
gives it colour,
the cold air feeds it.
No. The poem
after the poem,
the poem we're
heading towards
always, is the only
true poem, free
as a cliff of fulmar

to change shape,
to roost, to be forgotten,
to be silent; like the Arctic tern
to disappear in icy wastes
or there to be
augmented. So

6 a.m. and four of us up
and off on a caribou hunt.

III

We skirt the town and its graveyard of simple white crosses. Pack ice glows pink, green in the early morning light. Derek the hunter on lead skidoo zigzags across a gulley to get the lie of the land, then strikes out for the white nowhere. We ride along the top of a ridge, the top of the world, a lie that holds to the last moment when abruptly we're folded onto another one and another and another. I bounce on my skidoo, scream delight through my frozen balaclava, though at the same time feel I could let my head droop onto the handlebars, fall into the deepest of woolly sleeps.

We spot a frieze of caribou grazing snow over yet another rise – a herd of about a dozen a quarter of a mile away. Derek takes his rifle from its scabbard, climbs a rocky escarpment. A hollow thud without echo and a caribou drops while others scatter. The wounded caribou rises. Falls to its knees. The herd's confused, directionless. *Die, please die*, Leigh mutters. Derek on foot moves closer. I hold hunter and hunted in my gaze as he raises his rifle through a light glitter of snow. Then it's over and he's walking purposefully towards his kill. The only moving thing in all I see.

When we arrive on the skidoos the caribou, a female, is still twitching, a smear of blood from her stomach dripping onto the snow. *Just nerves*, Derek says. *She's dead*, passing an ungloved hand over her startled brown eyes and nostrils. But he jabs his short knife deep into her neck to make sure.

To work! She must be skinned and butchered before she freezes. He runs his knife up the inside of her legs, peels them; turns her onto her back; slits her arse to throat. Thrusting his hands deep into her warmth he eases the pepper and white hide down from the stomach and its crimson contents well out. At least he has missed the bladder where the Inuit believe the soul is seated. Skinned now, he hacks off the bony forelegs and tosses them into a pile of waste (on one hoof a trail of blood frozen dark as tar). *For the foxes*, he says. Into another pile, to be wrapped in the fresh skin and put in the sled, go the haunches, the strips of back, rump etc. Her innards, an intricately beautiful world of marble and root, pour out onto the bloodied snow. A foetus swells there: a kidney-shaped smoothness a couple of months from birth, it's a wonder her slight body could contain it. *Ah, we're makin her smaller now*, says Derek in his Newfoundland-Irish accent. *No, it's no sport this*, he says, stabbing at the neck to sever the head. *Here, stamp on these somebody*; he indicates the ribs with knife and fist the blood have almost made one. *Come on Derek*, I say, *let's see the foetus. We've seen everything else.*

Holding the haft loosely at its end, he swings the blade lightly through the sack and the amniotic fluid gushes out dampening the snow. He flicks the head out with the tip of his knife; the lilac body slithers after. Vegetable still, the ears are folded leaves, flat against the doglike head; soft hooves pointed like a bunch of purple iris heads, stems no thicker than the umbilical cord. We take this in in silence till Derek who's been rubbing his hands with snow says, *Oh I almost forgot – the tongue.* He picks the head up by a horn, slits the throat up-a-ways, lifts the tongue out and slices it off at root. *That one hurt*, says Leigh.

But there's something about the speed
with which the caribou becomes
food for us and food for foxes, the sureness
of Derek's touch in all he does –
even to the remembering
of that long tongue lolling from his fist –
that gives him a place on this blank page
below the clear blue sky: and that speaks,
strange though it may sound Bill,
of love.

The rest of us trap hot mugs of tea
in our hands; not a breath of wind
yet the cold stiffens us. Raising our mugs
we drink to the power
of his transforming art.

IV

I paw the ground
round the churned site
of the kill; rouse
below the thin snow crust
the raw smell
of earth, soon to be
graced with its carpet
of purple saxifrage,
buttoned by snow white avens.
Raising my head
I sniff
the air, the light; angle
an ear towards
silence.
    Beyond
the next silvery
blue ridge I sense
there's nothing
to hold me; though death
remains
historical, certified,
here on this stapled page,
love and memory
gather up the remains
where they lie
for all to find them
and tell
another story
in which the swan flies
over my head, the Inuit
comes home, the caribou
calves to the young boy's
delight; and you
brush that glitter of snow
from your shoulders
before the whisky's poured,
the tongue's loosened
and the story
begins.

Spring on the Prairie

When our crab apple tree showed the first
fingernails of green I pulled Julie across to look.
See! Spring's on its way. (Scottish subtext:

Winter's not for ever. Summer's a long way off yet,
a long hard road still to thole. But don't lose heart,
we're on our way.) Eight days later we returned

to bowers of green and the crab apple tree pouring out
its heart to us in clustering bulbs of light. Each park
had become a deep green lung and air

fresh as the sea washed all around us. Through it
our gestures to each other, to the world, flowed with poise
and grace, like the many hands of Ushnishasitatapattra –

the Tibetan goddess of wisdom and compassion whose image
(a gifted p.c.) sits on my desk. The night before we flew
for home I leant on a wire fence, my eyes grazing round

the park field whose winter snow was rarely tracked.
Now children like summer bees were everywhere, gorging
on freedom. In the neighbourhood ball game,

each team had their own wise, fair pitcher, who gently
lobbed the ball in a slow arch, his arm frozen
at each instant as Ushnishasitatapattra's are,

so that it was fair for young boys as it was
generous to the seasoned and skilled. With each thwack
summer stretched out, winter grew further away.

But such moments don't travel. We returned to grey skies,
to 'chilly for May', to good days to hang out the washing.
The briefest patch of blue now pulled from us

the most buoyant optimism. Our hearts bailed water,
hands flailing as we went down. Ushnishasita-
tatapattra, what a watery word you are now!

Then one evening, early, we leave a friend's house
for streets slightly damp with a rain too light
to notice. A rich aroma permeates the still warm air:

rhododendron, laburnum, lilac; but more than these,
the air itself is a bloom whose roots carry
down to the rich earth. And I remember

the pitcher's fluid arm, the evenness of each ball
as it arched through the air and fell
towards the drawn bat.

The Father

Our son breaks our sleep
with unconscious screaming: I don't
want to. I don't want to. I don't...

Want raspberry? Strawberry? This book
or that? So few real choices
he has in his life. I decide

to keep a small bag packed
for us both. When the time comes
I'll be ready. Sure enough

one evening, able to take no more
of our feeding patterns, he's off.
He's stronger than I thought

and more determined. In no time
we've cleared the last houses
and are in open country where

the whispering barley's ripe
for plucking; swifts dart in
shallow loops over our heads.

For some time we drift south,
taking lifts if we're offered
or looping back on our trail.

He's definitely getting used to
calling the shots: so some days
we'll be lions all day till my palms

ache; others spend by the roadside
piling stones till each cairn
casts its own tiny shadow

across his busy fists.
What we'll do when the money
runs out I haven't yet figured

but the nights grow warmer
and I find we need less and less.
Perhaps it seems strange to give

your life over to the whims
of a child, to spend it always
in the hinterland. Who can say

how it will work out or what
lessons, if any, we're learning?
Down among the blowsy poppies,

I disturb a wild bee
gorging at a daisy's heart.
It kicks out a yolkyellow leg

and I see him at his mother's
breast again, and think of
the distances we've travelled.

Tom Pow was born in Edinburgh in 1950. After studying at St Andrews and Aberdeen, he taught in Edinburgh, London and Madrid. He now lives in Dumfries with his wife and two children, and teaches in the English department of Dumfries Academy.

His first two collections of poetry, *Rough Seas* and *The Moth Trap* (Canongate), both received Scottish Arts Council Book Awards and *The Moth Trap* was shortlisted for Saltire Scottish Book of the Year. His third collection is *Red Letter Day* (Bloodaxe Books, 1996). He has travelled widely, and in 1992 published *In the Palace of Serpents: An Experience of Peru* (Canongate) which Ronald Wright, author of *Stolen Continents*, described as 'the most sensitive, wise and authentic "experience" I can remember reading on modern Peru'.

He is the author of two radio plays, *The Execution of Mary Timney* and *Wilderness Dreams*, and is currently working on his third for BBC Radio Four, *Aglooka: John Rae and the Fate of the Franklin Expedition*.

In his work as a teacher he is active in the promotion of Scots writing. He is the editor of *Shouting It Out* (Hodder and Stoughton), a collection of stories specially commissioned for teenagers and he has interviewed some of Scotland's most respected poets for Scottish Television's *In Verse*.

In 1992-93 he was holder of the Scottish/Canadian Fellowship, based at the University of Alberta.